WORDS OF WISDOM

Words of Wisdom
for the Bachelorette

Bryan J. Bohnert

iUniverse, Inc.
New York Lincoln Shanghai

Words of Wisdom
for the Bachelorette

Copyright © 2007 by Bryan J. Bohnert

All rights reserved. No part of this book may be used or reproduced by any means, graphic, electronic, or mechanical, including photocopying, recording, taping or by any information storage retrieval system without the written permission of the publisher except in the case of brief quotations embodied in critical articles and reviews.

iUniverse books may be ordered through booksellers or by contacting:

iUniverse
2021 Pine Lake Road, Suite 100
Lincoln, NE 68512
www.iuniverse.com
1-800-Authors (1-800-288-4677)

Because of the dynamic nature of the Internet, any Web addresses or links contained in this book may have changed since publication and may no longer be valid.

The views expressed in this work are solely those of the author and do not necessarily reflect the views of the publisher, and the publisher hereby disclaims any responsibility for them.

ISBN: 978-0-595-43046-8 (pbk)
ISBN: 978-0-595-68200-3 (cloth)
ISBN: 978-0-595-87390-6 (ebk)

Printed in the United States of America

This book, *Words of Wisdom for the Bachelorette*, is currently being compiled as a final wedding gift for our dearly beloved bachelorette, who is just hours away from tying the knot. However, this gift will not be complete without you.

Please turn to the next page, where you will find a numbered list of five very important questions. Read and select the question that you wish to offer your guidance on. Now turn the page. Write down the number of the question you will be answering, your first name, your age, the city and/or state in which you reside, and most importantly, a few words of wisdom for the bachelorette.

As you will note, we have not asked for your full name. Therefore we are asking that when leaving your words of wisdom for the bachelorette, you be as candid, sincere, and down-to-earth as possible. In other words, have fun!

You never know—five or ten years from now, when the owner of this book turns back to look for advice, it could be your words of wisdom that save her marriage.

Have fun, and happy writing!

WORDS OF WISDOM QUESTIONS

1. How can I show him that I love him?

2. How can I always make him feel sexy?

3. How can I keep from losing him?

4. How can I please him in the bedroom?

5. What should I <u>not</u> do in my marriage?

EXAMPLE

#4
Buy him a television for the bedroom! Trust me, it's well worth the investment and will keep you both happy in the long run.

Christy-30

Dallas, TX

Words of Wisdom
for the Bachelorette
From Your Maid Of Honor

3
Question Number

Love him for all his faults first everything else is a gift The presence

1. = Stand by his side.
2. - Give him sexy eyes lol!!
3. - Tell him "I ♥ you."
4. = B.J!!
5. - keep secrets

Lisa 33

Ray — 39   Chicago, IL

First Name   Age   City   State

Words of Wisdom

for the Bachelorette

\# _____
Question Number

A Blowjob everyday keeps the doctor away!

Jake + Casey

First Name — Age City, State

Words of Wisdom

for the Bachelorette

\# __3__
Question Number

Pretty sure this won't be a problem, but, worse comes to worse, chain him to the bed! That would prob. work too!

Rudd — 21
First Name — Age

Flotown, MO
City, State

Words of Wisdom

for the Bachelorette

5
Question Number

Never, never, never, ever criticize him in front of others! Always be tactful in how you share your concerns or problems with any issues in your marriage. Do everything you can to encourage him & NEVER discourage him. This will make him feel more like you recognize his wants and needs in your marriage.

Jackie — 30, St. Chuck, MO
First Name   Age   City   State

Words of Wisdom

for the Bachelorette

\# __6__
Question Number

ANSWER TO ALL QUESTIONS: GIVE HIM THE BUTT...!

BINDER / GREG — 26/24   O'FALLON, MO
First Name / Age   City   State

Words of Wisdom

for the Bachelorette

\# _____
Question Number

_____
_____
_____
_____
_____
_____
_____
_____
_____
_____

_____ - _____   _____ , _____
First Name   Age   City   State

Words of Wisdom

for the Bachelorette

\# _____
Question Number

_____
_____
_____
_____
_____
_____
_____
_____
_____
_____

_____-_____   _____,_____
First Name   Age   City   State

Words of Wisdom

for the Bachelorette

\# _____
Question Number

_____

_____

_____

_____

_____

_____

_____

_____

_____

_____

_____ - _____   _____ , _____
First Name   Age   City   State

Words of Wisdom

for the Bachelorette

\# _____
Question Number

_____
_____
_____
_____
_____
_____
_____
_____
_____
_____
_____

_____ - _____   _____ , _____
First Name   Age   City   State

Words of Wisdom

for the Bachelorette

\# _____
Question Number

_____

_____

_____

_____

_____

_____

_____

_____

_____ - _____   _____ , _____
First Name   Age   City   State

Words of Wisdom

for the Bachelorette

\# _____
Question Number

_____
_____
_____
_____
_____
_____
_____
_____
_____
_____
_____

_____ - _____   _____ , _____
First Name   Age   City   State

Words of Wisdom

for the Bachelorette

\# _____
Question Number

_____-_____ _____,_____
First Name   Age   City   State

Words of Wisdom

for the Bachelorette

\# __1__
Question Number

Always swallow.

Finn - 37
First Name / Age

Words of Wisdom

for the Bachelorette

2

Question Number

Tell him that he is the biggest you've ever had.

First Name - Age   City , State

Words of Wisdom

for the Bachelorette

\# __3__
Question Number

Make him feel like a King

Words of Wisdom

for the Bachelorette

\# __4__
Question Number

Heels and lingerie.

First Name — Age   City , State

Words of Wisdom

for the Bachelorette

\# __5__
Question Number

Words of Wisdom

for the Bachelorette

\# _____
Question Number

_____

_____

_____

_____

_____

_____

_____

_____

_____

_____-_____   _____,_____
First Name   Age   City   State

Words of Wisdom

for the Bachelorette

\# _____
Question Number

_____
_____
_____
_____
_____
_____
_____
_____
_____
_____

_____ - _____   _____ , _____
First Name Age   City   State

Words of Wisdom

for the Bachelorette

\# _____
Question Number

_____

_____

_____

_____

_____

_____

_____

_____

_____ - _____   _____ , _____
First Name   Age   City   State

Words of Wisdom

for the Bachelorette

\# _____
Question Number

_____
_____
_____
_____
_____
_____
_____
_____
_____

_____-_____   _____,_____
First Name   Age   City   State

Words of Wisdom

for the Bachelorette

\# _____
Question Number

_____
_____
_____
_____
_____
_____
_____
_____
_____

_____-_____ _____,_____
First Name   Age   City   State

Words of Wisdom

for the Bachelorette

\# _____
Question Number

_____
_____
_____
_____
_____
_____
_____
_____
_____
_____
_____

_____-_____   _____,_____
First Name   Age   City   State

Words of Wisdom

for the Bachelorette

\# _____
Question Number

_____

_____

_____

_____

_____

_____

_____

_____

_____

_____-_____   _____,_____
First Name   Age   City   State

Words of Wisdom

for the Bachelorette

\# _____
Question Number

_____-_____   _____,_____
First Name Age   City   State

Words of Wisdom

for the Bachelorette

\# _____
Question Number

_____
_____
_____
_____
_____
_____
_____
_____
_____
_____
_____

_____-_____   _____,_____
First Name   Age   City   State

Words of Wisdom

for the Bachelorette

\# _____
Question Number

_____ - _____ _____ , _____
First Name   Age   City   State

Words of Wisdom

for the Bachelorette

\# _____
Question Number

_____

_____

_____

_____

_____

_____

_____

_____

_____

_____-_____   _____,_____
First Name   Age   City   State

Words of Wisdom

for the Bachelorette

\# _____
Question Number

_____
_____
_____
_____
_____
_____
_____
_____
_____
_____
_____
_____

_____-_____   _____,_____
First Name   Age   City   State

Words of Wisdom

for the Bachelorette

\# _____
Question Number

_____

_____

_____

_____

_____

_____

_____

_____

_____

_____-_____   _____,_____
First Name   Age   City   State

Words of Wisdom

for the Bachelorette

\# _____
Question Number

_____
_____
_____
_____
_____
_____
_____
_____
_____
_____
_____

_____ - _____   _____ , _____
First Name   Age   City   State

Words of Wisdom

for the Bachelorette

\# _____
Question Number

_____

_____

_____

_____

_____

_____

_____

_____

_____

_____-_____   _____,_____
First Name   Age   City   State

Words of Wisdom

for the Bachelorette

\# _____
Question Number

_____
_____
_____
_____
_____
_____
_____
_____
_____
_____
_____
_____

_____-_____   _____,_____
First Name Age   City   State

Words of Wisdom

for the Bachelorette

_____
Question Number

_____
_____
_____
_____
_____
_____
_____
_____
_____
_____

_____ - _____   _____ , _____
First Name   Age   City   State

Words of Wisdom

for the Bachelorette

\# _____
Question Number

_____
_____
_____
_____
_____
_____
_____
_____
_____

_____-_____   _____,_____
First Name Age   City   State

Words of Wisdom

for the Bachelorette

\# _____
Question Number

_____
_____
_____
_____
_____
_____
_____
_____
_____
_____

_____-_____   _____,_____
First Name   Age   City   State

Words of Wisdom

for the Bachelorette

\# _____
Question Number

_____
_____
_____
_____
_____
_____
_____
_____
_____
_____
_____

_____ - _____   _____ , _____
First Name   Age   City   State

Words of Wisdom

for the Bachelorette

\# __3__
Question Number

Never, Never, Never go to bed mad at one another. Never, Never, Never get lazy with the way you look! Always look sexy for him.

Sheila — 38
First Name — Age

O'Fallon, MO
City — State

Words of Wisdom
for the Bachelorette

_____
Question Number

_____
_____
_____
_____
_____
_____
_____
_____
_____

_____ - _____   _____ , _____
First Name   Age   City   State

Words of Wisdom

for the Bachelorette

\# _____
Question Number

_____
_____
_____
_____
_____
_____
_____
_____
_____
_____

_____-_____   _____,_____
First Name   Age   City   State

Words of Wisdom

for the Bachelorette

\# _____
Question Number

_____
_____
_____
_____
_____
_____
_____
_____
_____
_____
_____

_____ - _____   _____ , _____
First Name   Age   City   State

Words of Wisdom

for the Bachelorette

\# _____
Question Number

_____
_____
_____
_____
_____
_____
_____
_____
_____
_____
_____
_____

_____-_____   _____,_____
First Name   Age   City   State

Words of Wisdom

for the Bachelorette

\# _____
Question Number

_____

_____

_____

_____

_____

_____

_____

_____

_____

_____ - _____   _____ , _____
First Name   Age   City   State

Words of Wisdom

for the Bachelorette

\# _____
Question Number

_____
_____
_____
_____
_____
_____
_____
_____
_____

_____-_____   _____,_____
First Name   Age   City   State

Words of Wisdom

for the Bachelorette

\# _____
Question Number

_____
_____
_____
_____
_____
_____
_____
_____
_____
_____

_____-_____ _____,_____
First Name Age   City   State

Words of Wisdom

for the Bachelorette

\# _____
Question Number

_____
_____
_____
_____
_____
_____
_____
_____
_____
_____

_____-_____ _____,_____
First Name Age   City   State

Words of Wisdom

for the Bachelorette

\# _____
Question Number

_____
_____
_____
_____
_____
_____
_____
_____
_____
_____
_____

_____ - _____   _____ , _____
First Name   Age   City   State

Words of Wisdom

for the Bachelorette

\# _____
Question Number

_____
_____
_____
_____
_____
_____
_____
_____
_____

_____-_____   _____,_____
First Name   Age   City   State

Words of Wisdom

for the Bachelorette

\# _____
Question Number

_____-_____ _____,_____
First Name   Age   City   State

Words of Wisdom

for the Bachelorette

\# _____
Question Number

_____
_____
_____
_____
_____
_____
_____
_____
_____

_____-_____   _____,_____
First Name Age   City   State

Words of Wisdom

for the Bachelorette

\# _____
Question Number

_____
_____
_____
_____
_____
_____
_____
_____
_____
_____

_____-_____   _____,_____
First Name   Age   City   State

Words of Wisdom

for the Bachelorette

\# _____
Question Number

_____

_____

_____

_____

_____

_____

_____

_____

_____

_____-_____   _____,_____
First Name   Age   City   State

Words of Wisdom

for the Bachelorette

\# _____
Question Number

_____

_____

_____

_____

_____

_____

_____

_____

_____

_____-_____   _____,_____
First Name   Age   City   State

Words of Wisdom

for the Bachelorette

\# 1,2,3,4,5
Question Number

Always be each others Best Friend. Be Honest, Be Open, Be Funny, Be Romantic. Don't be afraid to say your sorry. Always love your husband for who he is. Don't take each other for granted. Most of all Love Growing older together. My love and Best Wishes for many years of happiness together.

Martha — 53
First Name / Age

Dollar, The
City / State

Words of Wisdom

for the Bachelorette

\# _____
Question Number

_____
_____
_____
_____
_____
_____
_____
_____
_____
_____

_____-_____   _____,_____
First Name   Age   City   State

Words of Wisdom

for the Bachelorette

\# _____
Question Number

_____
_____
_____
_____
_____
_____
_____
_____
_____

_____-_____   _____,_____
First Name Age   City   State

Words of Wisdom

for the Bachelorette

\# _____
Question Number

_____
_____
_____
_____
_____
_____
_____
_____
_____

_____-_____   _____,_____
First Name Age   City   State

Words of Wisdom

for the Bachelorette

\# _____
Question Number

_____

_____

_____

_____

_____

_____

_____

_____

_____

_____-_____   _____,_____
First Name   Age   City   State

Words of Wisdom

for the Bachelorette

\# _____
Question Number

_____
_____
_____
_____
_____
_____
_____
_____
_____

_____-_____   _____,_____
First Name   Age   City   State

Words of Wisdom

for the Bachelorette

\# _____
Question Number

_____
_____
_____
_____
_____
_____
_____
_____
_____
_____

_____-_____ _____,_____
First Name   Age   City   State

Words of Wisdom

for the Bachelorette

\# _____
Question Number

_____
_____
_____
_____
_____
_____
_____
_____
_____
_____

_____-_____   _____,_____
First Name Age   City   State

Words of Wisdom

for the Bachelorette

_____
Question Number

_____

_____

_____

_____

_____

_____

_____

_____

_____

_____

_____-_____   _____,_____
First Name   Age   City   State

Words of Wisdom

for the Bachelorette

\# _____
Question Number

_____
_____
_____
_____
_____
_____
_____
_____
_____
_____

_____ - _____   _____ , _____
First Name Age   City   State

Words of Wisdom

for the Bachelorette

\# __3__
Question Number

Don'T Poke big bear with a stick when he is hung over and grumpy.
And always give him BUTT sex...... you not him (No strapons allowed) Just kidding

Best wishes Love you guys

Kevin - 45   O'Fallon, MO
First Name Age   City   State

Words of Wisdom

for the Bachelorette

\# __3__
Question Number

Lots & Lots & Lots & Lots & Lots of SEX! Monkey Sex: Hanging from Ceiling. Snow White Sex: In front of the Mirror Mirror. Hwy Sex: While driving down the road. Balcony Sex: Self explanatory and then at year number Seven, Spice it up and invite a friend.

BEST WISHES To You Both!

__Bryan__ - __41__
First Name / Age

__Wtz__, __MO__
City / State

P.S. Dont forget __69__ too!

Words of Wisdom

for the Bachelorette

\# _____
Question Number

_____
_____
_____
_____
_____
_____
_____
_____

_____-_____ _____,_____
First Name Age City State

Words of Wisdom

for the Bachelorette

\# _____
Question Number

_____
_____
_____
_____
_____
_____
_____
_____
_____
_____

_____-_____   _____,_____
First Name   Age   City   State

Words of Wisdom

for the Bachelorette

\# _____
Question Number

_____

_____

_____

_____

_____

_____

_____

_____

_____

_____-_____   _____,_____
First Name   Age   City   State

Words of Wisdom

for the Bachelorette

\# _____
Question Number

_____
_____
_____
_____
_____
_____
_____
_____
_____
_____

_____ - _____   _____ , _____
First Name   Age   City   State

Words of Wisdom

for the Bachelorette

\# _____
Question Number

_____

_____

_____

_____

_____

_____

_____

_____

_____

_____ - _____   _____ , _____
First Name   Age   City   State

Words of Wisdom

for the Bachelorette

\# _____
Question Number

_____

_____

_____

_____

_____

_____

_____

_____

_____

_____

_____-_____   _____,_____
First Name   Age   City   State

Words of Wisdom

for the Bachelorette

\# _____
Question Number

_____

_____

_____

_____

_____

_____

_____

_____

_____

_____-_____   _____,_____
First Name   Age   City   State

Words of Wisdom

for the Bachelorette

\# _____
Question Number

_____
_____
_____
_____
_____
_____
_____
_____
_____
_____

_____ - _____   _____ , _____
First Name   Age   City   State

Words of Wisdom

for the Bachelorette

\# _____
Question Number

_____
_____
_____
_____
_____
_____
_____
_____
_____

_____-_____   _____,_____
First Name Age   City   State

Words of Wisdom

for the Bachelorette

\# _____
Question Number

_____
_____
_____
_____
_____
_____
_____
_____
_____
_____

_____-_____   _____,_____
First Name Age   City   State

Words of Wisdom

for the Bachelorette

\# _____
Question Number

_____

_____

_____

_____

_____

_____

_____

_____

_____ - _____   _____ , _____
First Name   Age   City   State

Words of Wisdom

for the Bachelorette

\# _____
Question Number

_____

_____

_____

_____

_____

_____

_____

_____

_____

_____ - _____   _____ , _____
First Name   Age   City   State

Words of Wisdom

for the Bachelorette

\# _____
Question Number

_____

_____

_____

_____

_____

_____

_____

_____

_____-_____   _____,_____
First Name   Age   City   State

Words of Wisdom

for the Bachelorette

\# _____
Question Number

_____
_____
_____
_____
_____
_____
_____
_____
_____
_____

_____-_____   _____,_____
First Name   Age   City   State

Words of Wisdom

for the Bachelorette

\# _____
Question Number

_____

_____

_____

_____

_____

_____

_____

_____

_____

_____-_____   _____,_____
First Name   Age   City   State

Words of Wisdom

for the Bachelorette

\# _____
Question Number

_____
_____
_____
_____
_____
_____
_____
_____
_____
_____

_____-_____   _____,_____
First Name Age   City   State

Words of Wisdom

for the Bachelorette

\# _____
Question Number

_____-_____
First Name   Age

_____,_____
City   State

Words of Wisdom

for the Bachelorette

\# _____
Question Number

_____

_____ - _____   _____ , _____
First Name   Age   City   State

Words of Wisdom

for the Bachelorette

_____
Question Number

_____
_____
_____
_____
_____
_____
_____
_____

_____-_____   _____,_____
First Name   Age   City   State

Words of Wisdom

for the Bachelorette

\# _____
Question Number

_____
_____
_____
_____
_____
_____
_____
_____
_____
_____

_____-_____   _____,_____
First Name   Age   City   State

Words of Wisdom

for the Bachelorette

_____
Question Number

_____

_____

_____

_____

_____

_____

_____

_____

_____-_____   _____,_____
First Name   Age   City   State

Words of Wisdom

for the Bachelorette

\# _____
Question Number

_____

_____

_____

_____

_____

_____

_____

_____

_____ - _____   _____ , _____
First Name   Age   City   State

Words of Wisdom

for the Bachelorette

\# _____
Question Number

_____

_____

_____

_____

_____

_____

_____

_____

_____-_____   _____,_____
First Name   Age   City   State

Words of Wisdom

for the Bachelorette

\# _____
Question Number

_____

_____

_____

_____

_____

_____

_____

_____

_____

_____-_____   _____,_____
First Name   Age   City   State

Words of Wisdom

for the Bachelorette

\# _____
Question Number

_____
_____
_____
_____
_____
_____
_____
_____

_____-_____ _____,_____
First Name Age   City   State

Words of Wisdom

for the Bachelorette

\# _____
Question Number

_____
_____
_____
_____
_____
_____
_____
_____
_____
_____

_____-_____   _____,_____
First Name   Age   City   State

978-0-595-68200-3
0-595-68200-6

Printed in the United States
97593LV00004BB/7-15/A